PROVISIONS FOR YOUR PURPOSE

Adetola Balogun

Provisions For Your Purpose

For permission requests, enquiries, consultations, kindly contact the author via the following channel:

Email: adetola_balogun@yahoo.com

DEDICATION

I hereby dedicate this book to the glory of the Lord God Almighty, also to my Lord and Saviour Jesus Christ and the precious Holy-Spirit for keeping me for this few years on earth and helping to discover my purpose here on earth and to keep on fulfilling this assignment. I also dedicate this book to every human longing to know why they are on this earth. God brought you here for an assignment and He is always willing to satisfy that longing in your heart and empower you to fulfil your purpose.

CONTENTS

ACKNOWLEDGEMENTS

With special thanks to the Lord God the father of lights, our creator and also to my Lord and Saviour Jesus Christ and the precious Holy-Spirit for enabling me to write this book. I also thank my amiable wife Omolara for her relentless support and push, also to my darling children, Momoreoluwa and Moyinoluwa thank you for your care and love. I would also like to appreciate my extended family members too, God will reward you mightily in Jesus name. To my mentors, Pastor Noruwa E., Pastor Bachinobi U., Pastor F. Olaoye, Revd. Obioha, Pastor O. Oyebode, Mr Doyin Balogun and Mr Femi Akinbola to mention a few, thank you for your exemplary leadership and for showing us the way to improve always. Also not forgetting as many I have been privileged to impact and add value too on the way to the top.

May we truly know and walk in the purpose God our father has brought us forth into this world. Your season of manifestation truly awaits you!

PREFACE

In this book, we see that Our God is a God of purpose. He created all things for a reason. There is no mistake which he effected in creation. All creation created by Him has a purpose. The animals, trees, lands, the firmaments and so on have a purpose. Even we human beings which He created in His very own image and after His likeness have a purpose (Gen 1:25-26). We also need to know that the purpose of God for our lives is the reason and assignment that God has given us on earth. Our Lord Jesus Christ also who is our model had his own life's purpose which was to destroy the works of the devil and reconcile us to God (1 John 3:8, John 10:10b, Rom 5:21). This book was borne out of a desire to see all persons fulfil their purpose which can only in God. I had delayed this book writing for some few years before now until during the COVID pandemic then God gave me ability to pen down this thoughts. Every purpose of God for any individual cannot be achieved in isolation.

This book emphasizes that we can fulfil God's purpose through some provisions which we need to take cognisance and leverage on which are the provision of God Himself, the provision of helpers of our destiny and also the provision of God's precious promises. Also, when we live in the abundant life Jesus has given unto us we are also fulfilling our purpose.

I pray we will truly be blessed by reading and digesting this book in Jesus name. Shalom!

FOREWORD

In Acts 1:1 we see that Jesus began to do before he taught. Meaning that the teachings of Jesus were overflows from His faith based dealing with life. Unarguably, Jesus is the best teacher of all times being able to effectively breakdown ambiguous information of the kingdom into simple, practical and transmittable formats which has been proven true in all generations. The key being; **HE DID, THEN HE TAUGHT.**

Having known the author of this lovely book; Adetola Balogun for many years I can say he has systemically internalized this principle of Jesus to teach what he has seen, heard and handled with his hands concerning the word of life (1 John 1:1) . Therefore, I can say without doubt that the messages of this book are not coming from a loose canon but from a man who over the years have given himself to apply the word of God and have seen it work first hand and has therefore decided by the leading of the Spirit to share.

Beloved you are holding in your hands time proven principles of the kingdom which if you do well to apply will not only revolutionalize your life but also the lives of as many you'd share with because the principles of the kingdom will work in the hands of anyone who diligently applies their hearts to it.

Having been a teacher of the word myself for almost two decades now and written several books, I can tell you a good book when I see one. In this book you won't only be inspired but you shall also be activates to become all that God has ordained for you to become. Adetola Balogun wrote this book with was to read and understand lexicons, scriptures backed wisdom, real life stories and illustrations and sensational order that will leave you refreshed, refueled and refired to claim your purpose and identity in Christ Jesus.

I give you the book; provision for your purpose!

Get ready for revolution as you dive into the pages of this book.

CROWN OBIOHA is the senior pastor of SURECITY INTERNATIONAL CHRISTIAN CENTRE, Lagos.

ENDORSEMENTS

I have known Adetola Balogun from his teenage years and actually pastored him at some point in the teenage church. He has been a person of consistency and direction, one who listens and wants to learn.

Having gone through this book, I am not surprised this is coming from him. The book in itself is like a road sign, which is just a round or square board as a pole but has a lot of influence on all road users. Small, bride and easy to read, but yet filled with wisdom and direction.
A must read for teenagers!

Bachinobi Ufodike is currently the General Manager of TMX Nig. Ltd.

The MD/CEO of Highland B & C, The Advisory board chairperson of Jethro Leadership academy of RCCg LP77, An Area Pastor with RCCG, also a Fellow of the Institute of Management Consulting. Among other things.

I am very delighted o be writing this for Tola. I am not surprised that he has written a book. His hunger for God and the greater good of his neighbour is evident to all.

Well done Tola, I am very proud of you.
I recommend this book as a faith booster.

Noruwa Edokpolo
PICP RCCG LP77

I have know the Author of this inspiring book for over 10years and his trail has been marked with resilience, determination, wisdom , and the spirit of doing all he engages in with excellence. He is characterized as an insightful and passionate friend who supports others to attain their goals. Now I know that the foundation of what he does is rooted in discovering his purpose and absolute dedication to the things of God.

Dear Tola, this is to say thank you for submitting yourself to be an instrument to lead people to live their purpose.
I recommend this book to everyone desiring to have a realization of their purpose and live an impactful life through the help of the Holy spirit.

Olajumoke Agbelusi *Manufacturing Integration Director for Middle East and Africa, Philip Morris.*

Adetola has skillfully and gracefully elucidated on the topic of "purpose"... and why self discovery and the reason "why" is critical for fulfillment here on earth outlining steps to take and the benefits of taking responsibility..its a must read.

Mr Adedoyin Balogun, *MD/CEO Baldon Clothiers.*

Inspiring and challenging of the faith and phenomenal need to focus at believing and realising purpose.
You may find this book useful in connecting with destiny and appreciating the import of destiny helpers.
Adetola took time to drive strongly reality checks with his personal experience. Far reaching was his intent to share the impact of God

in directing and enabling seekers to embrace the path to purpose through the word of God.

I kindly recommend this Book.

Joshua Akinbanjo
Joshua is currently Senior Managing Partner at Number Quest Ltd,a Business Advisory and Brand Marketing Solutions firm. He was formerly Divisional Manager, Wear Africa at Coca-Cola Nigeria & Equatorial Africa, Head of Strategy & Promotions at Global, COO of The Creative Counsel, and Head, Account Management & Business Development at Insight Publicist.

INTRODUCTION

It is with great joy and all sense of humility that I write this book which the Lord God has laid in my heart for some three (3) years now, thank God I had the privilege to start writing this book in the midst of the pandemic in the year 2020.

This book will be an insight to everyone who has prayed, waited on the Lord and has been what the very cause of my existence on earth is! Now this brings us to the question what is purpose? Purpose is the reason for which something is done or created or for which something exists. All God's promises in the scriptures whether they be in the old or new testament are meant to be fulfilled in its season (Isa 34:6, Ps 40:8), this also includes us whom He created in His image, we must fulfil our very purpose according to what He has written concerning us (1 John 3 :8). It is also worthy of note that as many have received Jesus Christ into their lives are seeds of Abraham and heirs of the blessings, promises of God to Abraham (Gal 3:29). Are we really searching to know His promises unto us, for in His promises contains His will and our very purpose mandate which we have been ordained to walk in(1pet 1:3).

This book will by the Grace of God help us discover our very purpose for which we are been birthed and what He has provided for us to walk and achieve that purpose. God told our father Abraham that as far as his eyes can see so is He committed to given to him. Our father, Abraham truly fulfilled his purpose and was blessed as he walked with His creator and saw the invisible. We are also to walk in his stead of destiny fulfilment.

We will indeed fulfil and manifest according to what God has ordained for us in Jesus name.

Shalom!

CHAPTER 1

PROVISION OF HIMSELF

God has provided provisions of salvation for mankind. As it is written whosoever shall call on the name of the Lord shall be saved.

Dear friends, it is also written that no greater love than a man lay down his life for friends. (John 15:13) The Lord has sent his promises to us by Sending His Only begotten Son Jesus that if we receive Him we are assumed of eternal life(John 3:16).Oh what other promise can we ask for than when He(God) gives us himself Ps 50:14-15.

It is common knowledge to know that when a person gives up himself to an individual this is greatest show of love. It is also written in the Holy Scripture that with the provision of Jesus to as all other promises from God, He is ever willing to give to us (Romans 8:32.)

This means that God our father who spared not His son, but gave him up will with His son freely give us all things. Did we notice the sequence His Son was given to us first before any other thing else! This shows the import of a person's life Hallelujah!

Dear friends, I will like us to have this in mind that our father the Lord God Almighty loves us and the wants us so deeply to have an intimate relationship with us that was why he gave up his son and by extension himself for our salvation, every other thing in this life and in the life to come is ours provided we believe and accept we sacrifice of His begotten son (John 1:12-14).

Our father, Abraham showed us a shadow off things to come, when God told him to sacrifice his son Isaac, the only Son he had, he willingly did and we know what happened after. God told him He will bless Him and in multiplying He will multiply Him (Gen 22:1-19). we need to also yield ourselves to Him first before any other thing we do for His kingdom.

When we give our time, resources, money and energy to the advancement of his kingdom this is valuable and pleasing in His sight. Hallelujah!

We can't fulfil our purpose outside of not believing and receiving His Person into our lives first. It is after we receive the provision of Himself and believe His sacrifice for us and walk in that consciousness that we can have power to fulfil this eternal purpose (John 1:12-14, Rom 8:32) this cannot be more over emphasized again and again. The Lord God give us more understanding in Jesus name.

CHAPTER 2

PROVISION OF HELPER'S OF DESTINY

It is worthy of note and important to know that there is no self-made man in life. Everyone at sometime in his or her life has been helped or favoured by someone to achieve his God given purpose, our master the Lord Jesus while on earth at about age thirty (30) year when he was to fulfil His purpose had to choose twelve (12) persons which we know as His disciples today. These persons helped Him fulfil God's purpose and through them the gospel of the Lord Jesus Christ is reaching every part and the ends up the earth (mark 16:20).

Let us take another example of a helper of destiny which is Ananias and Paul (formerly called Saul of Tarsus). After Paul had an encounter with the Lord Jesus Christ on his away to Damascus he was suddenly blind as he had a personal encounter with Jesus when a bright light shone on him. The scripture says that he was blind for a season until the Lord Jesus spoke to a certain disciple named Ananias to go a particular area where Saul abode and have hands laid on Paul that he may receive his sight. Paul needed to have his sight regained so he might fulfil his purpose which was to take the gospel to the gentiles and the children of Israel (Acts 9:10-18), thank God for the disciple Ananias in the life of Paul who was his helper of destiny. I pay that your helper of destiny will encounter you speedily and will not rest until you are favoured and helped to achieve your purpose in Jesus name.

I will cite a personal example in my life, a personal example of one of helpers of my destiny is my Dad of blessed memory **Pastor Anthony Adetayo Balogun** he helped me as a little child attain my destiny by always pushing me to love the things and service of God as per Kingdom work. I remember at a particular time as a teenager who was still looking for admission into university he instructed that I must make sure we were part of those who cleaned the house of God every Saturday so that church on Sunday was always tidy and in order. I and my siblings did not have a weekend as it was for the work of God always during that time. Those times were inconvenient. There was a time my Dad opted that church musical instruments which were very heavy will be kept in our house so every Sunday morning as early as past 5am we had to bath and start morning Church Musical instruments from the house to his car then we moved it to church and offloaded them this happened for several months before the church resolved the issue and built a good store house for the equipment, by the grace of God today I am a teacher of the word in God's Kingdom and happily blessed. I have never known a better last year (prov. 4:18).

I will also cite another personal example of a helper of destiny my brother **Mr Adedoyin Balogun** he among others was one of these instruments in helping me through the university. I recall after he just got married a year after to be precise, I just got an admission into a private university and the fees were on the high side. After my Dad and Mum would gather the school fees money they could, my brother and his wife would make sure every year he they would also help send a large chunk of money too to assist my Dad in providing the school fees this happened for five (5) years in my stay in the university. I pray for someone today that the helpers of your destiny would not rest until they locate you and show you mercy and favour in Jesus name.

The Apostle Paul in his letter to the church at Corinth also told us of a very great helper of his destiny which is the **Grace of God** in (2 Cor. 15:10), he said I am what I am by the Grace of God. The Grace of God is also a channel, a very important channel to help a individual fulfil his/her destiny.

Even Jesus had Grace and Favour with God and men Mark 2:40,52 thank God for the Grace of God as a helper of destiny. David and Jonathan is another classical example in the Bible of those that are sent to help one achieve his destiny and purpose in life. Jonathan and David were closely knitted friends, the bible records that Jonathan who was king Saul's son delighted much in David and Jonathan told David when his father Saul was seeking to kill David(1sam 19:1-17).

David and Jonathan were so closely knitted that Jonathan showed David all things. Jonathan was truly a helper of destiny to David that on many instances he would have been killed on his way to fulfilling destiny and purpose, thank God he sent him destiny helpers I decree just like Jonathan was to David that men and women from all facets of life would just help you get to your place God has ordained for your life. They will reveal to you the enemies secrets which you can leverage on to fulfil your destiny and purpose gloriously in Jesus name. Thanks God for helpers of destiny. I also will give another example of destiny of helpers in my own life, during my national Youth Service Corps I had the privilege of serving in the northern part of the country to be precise Paiko Minna, Niger state. I actually did not want to spend twelve months in that state but fate happened and all opportunities to leave the state as per redeployment did not succeed. In Paiko Niger state had the privilege of being with a church for worship and regular weekly service but the Pastor there tasked we with several activities and asked if i was just a member of the Church in Lagos where I came from my answer to him was no i wasn't and he actually said he knew this from my behaviour.

To cut the long story short the pastor gave me the opportunity to pastor a small church which was under the one he pastored for several months. This I was able to do with God's grace and help for a couple of months till i finished my natural Youth Services duration. Those months helped me nurture my teaching ability and skills and help me confirm that God had called me into the teaching ministry, I praise the LORD God for that situation I passed through. My friends, my prayer for you as you read his book is that God will set you up with persons or an individual who will be highly instrumental in fulfilling your God when purpose in Jesus name.

Remember if our Lord Jesus needed the twelve disciples to bring God's Kingdom on earth and fulfil His purpose triumphantly we truly need helpers of destiny. Think and ask the Lord God for helpers of destiny as they are all around and real.

Even the Apostle Paul formerly called Saul of Tarsus had different destiny helpers who were provided for him at his stage of his fulfilment of his God given purpose which Jesus had ordained for Him after the encounter with Jesus on the way to Damascus.

In career, business, politics, academics and every sphere of life there are helpers of destiny. We need to continually ask Him to open our eyes to see the calling and purpose He has ordained for us and ask Him to see the people He has positioned for us to help us fulfil His purpose victoriously in Jesus name. I also want to say that when the most high God has opened to you a great and effectual door which we can walk through to fulfil our purpose and He has shown you His purpose all hell and forces of darkness will be present to withstand your from fulfilling that destiny. Apostle Paul said a great and effected door is opened to me but there are many adversaries .So we need to keep pressing on and trusting God who has given His a purpose for our lives to make us victorious indeed.

It is also very important to note that as we move on to fulfil our purpose here on earth there will be a process we must pass through. We must trust God that he will take us through this process and glorify His name. There is a process through God will take in individual through some phase in life as He prepares the individual for his purpose. There are very many examples in the scriptures of this process through which God took some persons. Our father Abraham, Joseph, Daniel, King David even our very brother and Lord Jesus all had through go through a process even when they had a clear purpose of what the Almighty God wanted them to do in their generation.

My dear friend I pray that God will take every one of us through the process triumphantly and this very process will announce us to our world to God's Glory in Jesus name.

There are truly provisions for our purpose whether it be to fulfil our career, ministry, or every facet of our lives.

I recall a phase and time in my life where I had to trust God to come through for me in providing a job just when I finished my National Youth Service Corps (N.Y.S.C) as it is called in Nigeria West Africa. Shortly before I finished NYSC I began applying and been confident I would get a job placement in a multinational company. Things did not plan out that way I waited for a while after doing my N.Y.S.C. and was still applying all to no success. Even people which included family and friends who promised me job placements before I finished the N.Y.S.C. program those who asked I bring my resume and as God would have it nothing came from them. Alas, a fateful period came where after so much applying and attending several interview I just told God to just favour me to get a job placement and trusted Him.

Behold I got two job placements by God's mercy and favour to His Glory praise the Lord. It is my sincere prayer for someone reading this book who has trusted the Lord Almighty that indeed God will give answer to your very requests so you can truly fulfil your purpose in Jesus name. My friend as you begin to trust God for His help and favour this season He will come through for you. He alone will do what you believe Him for so you can fulfil your purpose in grand style. Glory! God has since then been placing helpers of destiny my path as I trust Him to fulfil my purpose in life.

CHAPTER 3

Provisions of His Precious Promises

God's precious promises are in his word. His word is forever settled in heaven, this means God's word can never fail (Isa40:8, Ps119:89). We will be looking at how God has provided his Precious promises as a pathway to fulfilling our God's given purpose. Let me also add to that when you see your purpose in his word which contains his precious promises then God our father is then committed to helping you fulfill it. The question is what are you seeing in His word?. God told our father Abraham as far as his eyes could see he was committed to given him(Gen13:14).
The scripture says whereby are given unto us exceeding great and precious promises; that by these(promises)ye might be partakers of the divine nature, having escaped the corruption that is in the world through lust.(2pet 1:3).God has truly provided for us His promises which are contained in his word to us so we can truly fulfill our purposes.

Our Lord Jesus Himself who is the word had a purpose, which scripture told us he came to deliver the world from sin and also to destroy the works of the devil(John1:29,1John3:8). All these purposes were also spoken in the Old Testament by the prophets concerning Him. My friend, Jesus through God's promises was able to key into His purposes. My dear friend, God's promises are contained in his infallible word which is given unto us we need to keep searching and reading ,meditating on his word then revelation will come unto us by his help to key into our purpose in Jesus name .

The Promised Holy Spirit

The most important thing for us as believers is to know that the Holy spirit is the promised Spirit of God for every believer that receives Jesus into his heart (John1:12,Eph1:13).

Oh my! We need the spirit of God which is the promised Holy Spirit every moment of our lives because without him we can't fulfill our purpose.

Even our Lord Jesus had an infilling of the Holy Spirit of God in Him for his purpose to be accomplished.(Acts10:38).Dear friend, when our Lord Jesus was to depart he told his disciples to wait in Jerusalem until they were endowed with power from on high, this he meant they should wait in Jerusalem till the Holy spirit come on them mightily. Jesus told them he would not leave them comfortless he would send the promised Holy Spirit from God so they could accomplish the task of doing their very assignments.(John16:13).

We then see ordinary men like Peter, James, John and they who the Holy spirit came on them been used mightily and accomplished what God had said they will do from the foundation of the world to His praise and glory .Please note, let us to keep being thirsty and keep seeking the Holy Spirit and He will fill us up to overflowing for our purpose to be accomplished in Jesus name(Eph5:18, Isa 44:3).

The Promise of Health (sound health) and Prosperity.
The Lord God has also provided His promises of sound health so we can fulfill our purpose too. He says in 3John1:2"beloved I wish above all things that thou mayest prosper even as your soul prospereth". It's important to know that a sound and healthy mind is very pertinent in accomplishing our God given assignment. Even Jesus spoke about God the father preparing a body for Him on the earthly needs to do fulfil His purpose. I pray God's healing now, upon your body, soul and spirit by the stripes of Jesus you are healed in every area of your life even as you read this book in Jesus name. Jesus's beating, scourging, chastisement and stripes bring forth your sound health now in Jesus name.(Isa 53:5,1pet2:24).

God is also after our prosperity. He wants us his people and children to fulfill our purpose and prosper greatly. Our lord Jesus become poor so we through his poverty might become rich.
This means we are to enjoy prosperity in every area of our lives as we fulfill our purpose,(2cor8:9,John10:10).
We really need to walk in this knowledge and victory over poverty in Jesus name. God helping us we will walk in this victory.

The Promise of Helps
The Lord God has promised us His help for our purpose and assignment on earth. It cannot be overemphasized the need for help in our life's journey and purpose fulfilment. As I have talked in the previous chapter on helpers of destiny I also want to talk about God promise in sending us his help for our life's purpose. But then, Israel my servant, Jacob whom I have chosen, the seed of Abraham my friend fear thou not, for I am with thee be not dismayed for I

am thy God. I will strengthen thee; yea I will help thee; yea I will uphold thy right hand of righteousness (Isa 41:8-10).Oh! What a reassuring statement from the Lord God as he has promised to help us. The scripture says that whosoever is of Christ is a seed of Abraham(Gal3:29).So for all Christians who belong to Christ we can be sure this promise of help from God the father is also our portion, we need to keep on confessing and believing this promise. Some of the reasons God has promised to help us is because he knows that there will surely be adversaries on our path to fulfilling our life's purpose and also our God given purpose which he has showed us can be frightening and discouraging because it is bigger than ourselves. We can begin to ask Oh God how I fulfil this very great vision or assignment. In the scripture we can see men like Joseph, David, Joshua, Gideon who God had to ensure them that he will send His help to them and even our Lord Jesus our Saviour had God's help(Lk2:40,52). My dear friends, once again please keep confessing and believing God for his help from above.(Heb 13:6,Ps54:4,Ps30:10).

I pray for you that indeed the Lord God Almighty will strengthen and help you will be marvellously to fulfil your purpose to the Glory of God, Amen!. We can also be reminded that the Holy Ghost which is given to every Christian at salvation is a great helper. Jesus told us He will send the Holy Ghost and will be a helper to us on our life's journey. So we can always engage to the help of the Holy Ghost.

I pray the Holy Ghost will continue to help us in every area of our lives and he will ultimately help us to fulfil the purpose God has created us which he has ordained before the foundation of the world. **Glory!**

The Promise of His never failing Word

God's word has been in existence since the beginning (john1:1). God so highly exalts his word above all his names (ps138:2). God is always committed to his word(Isa55:10-11,Num23:19)."God is not a man that he should lie neither is he the son of man that he should repent; has he spoken and would he not make good His promise". Dear friends, it is important to know what God word says concerning your purpose. Still looking at the case study of our father Abraham, God told him to leave his father's house to a place he will show him and that He (God) would make him great. After Abraham had many encounters with the Lord God and His word, God also assured him that as far as his eyes can see what He is saying, he God is committed to seeing to him. **Glory!**. This means if we can see deep revelations our purpose in his word that never fails God himself who honours his word above all his name is committed to fulfilling it.(Jer1:12). The question to us then is are we seeing our very purpose in God's word? (Gen13:14,Isa 55:10-11). I pray we start to see beyond the physical by revelation in God's word, who we truly are and He(GOD) empowers us to fulfil our God given purpose. Even our Lord Jesus on many occasions would always assure his disciples that as the father sent Him to fulfil his purpose so he also send his disciples and us too by extension. **Glory!.**

I pray God's word spoken into our lives will be fulfilled in its time in Jesus name. We will truly fulfil our God given purpose as we see deep revelations in God's word about us. We however need to keep reading, studying and meditating of God's word(John1:8, Isa 34:16)

- **The promise of access to Christ's finished work**- Dear friend, our Lord and Saviour Jesus Christ, said it is finished when he hung in the cross and was crucified. His life on earth, death, burial and resurrection truly was not in vain because it had its significance (John 11:30). It is also worthy of note to know that Jesus said His coming was for all men to have life and have it more abundantly (John10:10b). Jesus said "the thief cometh not but to steal, kill and destroy but I am come that ye may have life and have it more abundantly." When we walk in the abundant life that Christ accessed for us we will definitely walk in our purpose. I pray that indeed we have access into the abundant life Jesus Christ accessed for us thereby fulfilling our purpose. We will continue to look at the various things Jesus has given us access freely into however not exhaustively.
- **We are more than conquerors in Him (Rom8:37)**- Through Jesus we are truly more than conquerors. Who is a conqueror?- A conqueror is one who has fought and won a battle. Jesus Christ defeated Principalities, powers, and rulers of darkness in high places and of course the devil our adversary and is seated for above all of them. I spoke earlier about when a man is empowered to fulfill his destiny there will surely be opposition or enemies. The enemies can be the host of hell let loose against him. Thank God Jesus has secured victory for us with us even fighting .All we need to do is to position ourselves and receives by faith this victory thereby we been more than conquerors.
- **We are blessed with every spiritual blessings in Him (Eph1:3)**-The scripture says that blessed be the Lord who has blessed us with all spiritual blessings in Christ Jesus

This means in Christ Jesus we have access to every blessing that will make us attain the full measure of Christ Jesus. What is a blessing? we see blessings in the life of our father Abraham where God told that in him all the nations of the earth will be blessed. A blessing is a force which causes good things in nature to help a man fulfill his purpose. God told Abraham that in blessing, he will bless Abraham and in multiplying he will multiply our father Abraham. Our father Abraham truly fulfilled his purpose because of the blessing of the God at work in his life (Gen12:1-2).

Dear friend, I pray for you that the blessings of the Lord which is in Christ Jesus will be freely accessed by you in Jesus name thereby you fulfilling your purpose in Jesus name. A man can't truly fulfill his purpose if he not blessed from above. Dear friend you will truly access the blessings of the Lord God and our father, Abraham in Jesus name(Gal3:29).

- **We have access into unsearchable riches of Christ**- Dear friend, in Christ Jesus we have access into deep riches. The bible says that we know the Grace of our Lord Jesus Christ that though he was rich, he became poor for our sakes so that through his poverty we might become rich (2 Cor8:9). In Christ Jesus, we have access into riches, not just riches, unsearchable riches of Jesus Christ. When we talk of riches, riches have different areas, there is an adage that says "health is wealth or riches" Riches is not only having plenty in goods and money but been prosperous in body, spirit and soul (3John1:2). The Greek word translated"unsearchable" describes something that cannot be fully comprehended or explored. In other words, there is no limit to the riches of Christ, they are past finding out (Rom 11:33). We can try to dig deep, but we can never plumb into the depth of Christ's worth. The Apostle Paul by revelation showed us some of these riches which are redemption through his blood, the forgiveness of sins, the knowledge of life mystery of his will, the message of truth, the empowerment and infilling of the Holy spirit the guarantee of our inheritance and live eternal life in him. The list above can't be exhausted but as the Holy spirit reveals more to us, we will definitely ride and walk into this access(1Cor2:9-10). All these privileges in Christ Jesus are necessary for us to fulfill our purpose(s) in grand style as it equips us fully. The Lord God through the finished works of Jesus Christ grant us access into the unsearchable riches of Christ Jesus thereby causing us to find and walk in our purpose and finish well in Jesus name.

❖ **We receive healing for our bodies**- A prepared body is also important for us to fulfill our purpose, when your body is not whole for example when we fall into diseases or sickness we can't truly fulfill our purpose. Thank God for his grace, however we can also key into the healing stripes of Jesus and access our healing by the faith and confession (1Pet2:24, Isa53:5). The first man (Adam) was full of sin, sickness and disease and became common to us. We thank God however for Jesus (the second Adam) his healing stripes, his chastisement, his body broken brought us divine healing. This is necessary for our walk on earth and purpose fulfillment. Even our Lord and Savior Jesus knew that God had to prepare him a body free of sickness and diseases. Dear friend, I pray even as you live in this body on earth the healing stripes of Jesus perfect your health, remove sickness and diseases from your body now in Jesus name. Be healed in Jesus name so you can be empowered to fulfill your purpose. Shalom!

Also the scripture says **in (2 cor 7:1) having these promises, dearly beloved, let us cleanse ourselves from all filthiness of the flesh and spirit,perfecting holiness in the fear of God.** This means that as we seek to fulfil our purpose and God's promises to us, we make sure we please God and live holy we should be careful not displease Him. We should seek to be righteous, holy and be obedient to Him always and ask for His mercy and blood to cleanse us from all unrighteousness when we sin and err . This will help our purpose fulfilment to be glorious and colourful.

Theme of Song
LORD I AM AVAILABLE FOR YOU.

Lord, I am available for you.

My will, I give to you.

I'll do what you say do, use me Lord.

To show someone the way and enable me to say;

My storage in empty and I am available for you (2X).

Theme of Song
COLOURFUL AND IT'S BRIGHT I WILL GET THERE.

Colourful and it's bright I will get there (2X).

My future is bright I will get there (2X).

Colourful and it's bright I will get there (2X).

My purpose is bright I will get there (2X).

SUMMARY

As believers' in Christ Jesus we truly need to come up higher and seek earnestly to fulfill our purpose(s). Our Lord Jesus and a host of witnesses are cheering us up to walk in the abundant life he has given us thereby fulfilling our purpose(s). As it is written the whole world is waiting for our manifestation as sons of God (Rom8:19, LK4:14).

God has truly provided a lot for us to walk in our purpose fulfillment in grand style, however we need to see this provision, key into it prayerfully and go forth with action and faith.

If Jesus, through the help of the Holy Spirit could fulfill his purpose on earth we also need the precious Holy Spirit because with Him comes other things in aiding our purpose fulfilment (Rom 8:32). Our existence and purpose is found in the creator and by yielding and trusting Him to walk in it.

I pray that henceforth as we believe and trust Him we will live nothing less of our purpose in Jesus name (John 10:10, 1John 3:8). You will surely fulfill your purpose and destiny thereby glorifying Jesus and the lord God Almighty in Jesus name. **Shalom!**

Did you also know that our very ultimate eternal purpose of existence is to praise and glorify the Lord God our creator? Yes, this is what we will be doing throughout all eternity just enjoying God's presence and praising Him with all the angels too. **Halleluyah!** (I Tim 1 :17, Psa 115:18, Rev 5:13).

Come up higher and fulfill you very purpose in Jesus name the whole earth is awaiting your manifestation!

If you haven't received the Lord Jesus, I urge you to do that right now, please say Lord Jesus I thank you for dying on the cross for me, I thank you for burial and resurrection and what it did for me. I receive you into my heart as my Lord and personal savior in Jesus name, amen. (Rom 10:9-10).

PRAYERS

1. **Father, I thank you for showing me in your mercy that you want me to fulfil my purpose and not die unfulfilled in Jesus name.**
2. **Father, please by your mercy empower me to fulfil my purpose and truly manifest as your son/daughter in this world in Jesus name.**
3. **Father, please let my light shine forth indeed and let your purpose concerning me truly be fulfilled in Jesus name.**
4. **Father, please open my eyes and empower me to walk in the abundant life that Jesus has secured for me in Jesus name.**
5. **Father, please by your mercy and grace help me to please you in all that I do henceforth in Jesus name.**
6. **Almighty God, Abba Father please help me to have access into the unsearchable riches of Christ Jesus so I can fulfil my purpose triumphantly in Jesus name.**
7. **Father, please all that you have provided for me on earth to fulfil my purpose, I pray that I will not miss out on them, I will truly utilize them and be fruitful to the glory of your name in Jesus name.**
8. **Father, I thank you because by your grace and mercy I and all my household will be in the center of your plan and purpose for our lives and we will praise you continually throughout eternity in Jesus name.**

www.ingramcontent.com/pod-product-compliance
Lightning Source LLC
LaVergne TN
LVHW012034160826
845678LV00013B/2586

* 9 7 8 9 7 8 9 9 1 6 2 4 5 *